ENDANGERED WILDLIFE

Barbara J. Behm
Jean-Christophe Balouet

Gareth Stevens Publishing
MILWAUKEE

▲▽

For a free color catalog describing Gareth Stevens' list of high-quality books, call 1-800-542-2595 (USA) or 1-800-461-9120 (Canada). Gareth Stevens' Fax: (414) 225-0377.

The editor would like to extend special thanks to Jan W. Rafert, Curator of Primates and Small Mammals, Milwaukee County Zoo, Milwaukee, Wisconsin, for his kind and professional help with the information in this book.

Library of Congress Cataloging-in-Publication Data

Behm, Barbara J., 1952-
    Endangered Wildlife/by Barbara J. Behm and Jean-Christophe Balouet.
      p.   cm. — (In peril)
    "Adapted from Ces espèces qui disparaissent . . . with original text by Jean-Christophe Balouet"—T.p. verso.
    Includes bibliographical references (p. 30) and index.
    ISBN 0-8368-1077-5
    1. Endangered species—Juvenile literature.   2. Wildlife conservation—Juvenile literature. [1. Endangered species. 2. Wildlife conservation.] I. Balouet, Jean-Christophe. Ces espèces qui disparaissent. II. Title. III. Series: Behm, Barbara J., 1952- In peril.
    QL83.B45   1994
    591.52'9—dc20   9411677

This edition first published in 1994 by
Gareth Stevens Publishing
1555 North RiverCenter Drive, Suite 201
Milwaukee, Wisconsin 53212, USA

Picture Credits
© 1993 Nate Bacon: p. 20; J. C. Balouet (with the courtesy of the Amphibians and Reptiles Laboratory of the National Museum of Natural History of Paris): p. 16 (lower); Botanical Conservatory of Brest: p. 26 (lower); Roger Bour: pp. 7 (lower), 23; Central Library Museum, National Museum of Natural History of Paris: pp. 8, 17, 22; CIRIC: p. 27; Explorer: pp. 9, 10, 12, 13, 25; © Ron Romanosky/Greenpeace: p. 14 (left); Jacana: Cover, pp. 15, 21 (both), 24, 28; Courtesy of Merck & Co., Inc. and the Institute for Biological Diversity (INBio): p. 19; Milwaukee Public Museum: p. 5; National Library: p. 7 (upper); Photo Researchers: p. 26 (upper); Douglas Pratt: p. 14 (right); Sipa: pp. 11, 18; Sky Raft: p. 6 (right); Vincennes Zoo: p. 6 (left)

Series logo artwork: Tom Redman

Series editor: Patricia Lantier-Sampon
Series designer: Karen Knutson
Research assistant: Derek Smith
Translated from the French by: Anne-Marie Jardon-Sampont
Additional picture research: Diane Laska
Map art: Donna Genzmer Schenström, University of Wisconsin-Milwaukee Cartographic
    Services Laboratory

Printed in the United States of America
1 2 3 4 5 6 7 8 9 99 98 97 96 95 94

INTRODUCTION

For millions of years, during the course of evolution, hundreds of plant and animal species have appeared on Earth, multiplied, and then, for a variety of reasons, vanished. We all know of animals today — such as the elephant and the rhinoceros, the mountain gorilla and the orangutan — that face extinction because of irresponsible human activity or changes in environmental conditions. Amazingly, hundreds of species of insects and plants become extinct before we can even classify them. Fortunately, in modern times, we are beginning to understand that all living things are connected. When we destroy a plant species, we may be depriving the world of an amazing cure for human diseases. And we know that if we destroy the forest, the desert creeps forward and the climate changes, wild animals die off because they cannot survive the harsh conditions, and humans, too, face starvation and death. Let us remember that every creature and plant is part of a web of life, each perfect, each contributing to the whole. It is up to each of us to end the destruction of our natural world before it becomes too late. Future generations will find it hard to forgive us if we fail to act. No matter what our age or where we live, it is time for every one of us to get involved.

Dr. Jane Goodall, Ethologist

CONTENTS

Words that appear in the glossary are printed in **boldface** type the first time they occur in the text.

ENDANGERED WILDLIFE

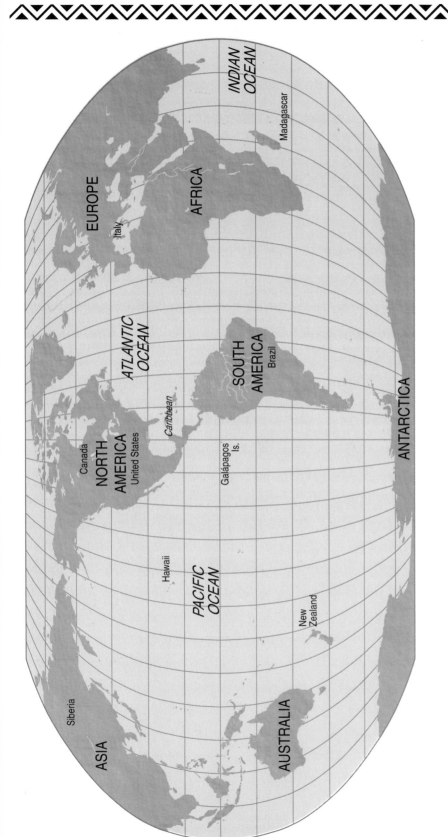

▲ For various reasons, many species of plant and animal life on Earth are in great peril of disappearing forever. Unfortunately, this danger is not limited to any one place; it has become a global problem. From the northern and southern continents to the islands and the oceans and seas, a long list of irreplaceable animal species needs the help and protection that only human resources can now provide. This map indicates some of the specific continents, countries, islands, bodies of water, and other world areas referred to in *In Peril: Endangered Wildlife*.

A CRY FOR HELP

"If the beasts were gone, men would die from great loneliness of spirit," said American Indian Chief Sealth. The leader of the Duwamish tribe spoke those words in 1885. Even then, he realized the importance of conserving the animals that live among us. Today, his words are more desperately true than ever.

Experts believe that half the animal and plant **species** presently living on Earth will be gone by the end of the twenty-first century. Estimates for this range between 500,000 and 2 million species. Imagine what it would be like to live in a world without animals and the bountiful **habitats** in which they make their homes. How cold a world it would be.

▲ American Indians hunted in earlier times, but they took only what they needed to survive.

Many hundreds of species of the world's animals are presently **endangered**. Endangered animals are those whose numbers are so low that they are in danger of becoming **extinct**. There are over nine hundred species of animals worldwide currently listed as endangered or threatened to become endangered in the future. The possibility of losing them is alarmingly real.

▲ This sky raft helps researchers keep track of animals in the wild.

▲ The Vincennes Zoo in Paris, France, shelters the last two known broad-nosed gentle lemurs.

LOST FOREVER

Once a species is lost, no amount of technology can replace it. Once a species is lost, it is lost forever.

It is already too late for many of the world's animals. Three hundred years ago, the

▲ Hundreds of bird species are threatened with extinction.

buffalo-like aurochs became extinct. Two hundred years ago, birds called dodos and the Carolina parakeets disappeared. One hundred years ago in New Zealand, the last Stephen Island wren died, a victim of the lighthouse keeper's cat.

Also gone are the passenger pigeon, the ruffed lemur, the Florida black wolf, and the great auk. Over the last two hundred years in the United States alone, forty bird

▲ The Réunion Island gecko is near extinction because of habitat destruction.

species, thirty-five mammal species, and twenty-five other animal species have become extinct. Many more species worldwide have not been observed for years and years, and they may be extinct. Such is the case with several Caribbean reptiles that have not been observed for the last twenty-five years.

AT THE EDGE OF EXTINCTION

The list of animals at the edge of extinction is growing at an astonishing rate. Included are the giant panda, the African and Asian elephants, the European red kite, the Asiatic lion, the Bengal and Siberian tigers, the orangutan, the mountain gorilla, the whooping crane, the red wolf, the California condor, the muriqui, the Florida manatee, the black-footed ferret, the peregrine falcon, the Atlantic salmon, several Brazilian monkeys, and the blue whale . . . just to name a very few.

▲ The forest homes of the endangered muriqui are destined for destruction.

One famous example is Lonesome George, a 134-year-old turtle that lives on the Galápagos Islands. Lonesome George is the last surviving member of a species of land turtle called *Chelonoidis abingdoni*. At one time, there were fifty-five land turtle species. By 1988, however, only eleven species still existed. Among these, four are listed as endangered.

THE FIGHT FOR LIFE

Species may become extinct because they cannot adapt properly, or keep up with the constantly changing conditions of their everyday existence. A very long time ago, some species of wildlife may have died out because of "natural" changes in the environment, such as a drop in sea level, a comet or asteroid crashing to Earth, or cooling temperatures. But by far, the greatest threats to wildlife today are the result

▲ This land, at one time, was lush and fertile. Human settlement forced too many animals to graze in a small area, and the land has become a useless desert.

▲ A once pure and beautiful beach is now polluted. Pollution destroys the environment for people as well as for wildlife.

of actions by people. Changes in the environment due to human intervention can be so drastic that wildlife and plant species are devastated. Humans number 5.5 billion worldwide. And studies show that, at the current rate of growth, the human population is expected to double in the next forty years! We, as a people, require food, water, shelter, and land. Our needs take up more and more of Earth's resources and habitat every day, destroying any nonhuman species that get in the way.

LOSS OF HABITAT

The most serious danger wildlife face today is loss of habitat. Habitat is lost when people clear the land for farms, cattle ranches, timber, and residential and industrial development; and when they build dams and drain wetlands. Developers destroy 300,000 acres (120,000 hectares) of wetlands each year in the United States alone. All these activities destroy the homes, feeding

▲ A rhinoceros is led away to a **reserve** where it will live peacefully, far from hunters.

▲ If destruction of the rain forest continues at the current rate, it will soon be gone.

insect species and 90 percent of the primate species live there. Millions of animal species would be lost.

This destruction affects humans, as well. Losing so many species could mean depriving the world of cures for all types of diseases. And when the land is cleared of forests, the climate eventually changes, and the land becomes a desert. Plants and animals that once thrived in the habitat die off. Because all the natural resources are gone, humans who live there cannot survive either.

areas, and breeding sites of wildlife.

About 50 million acres (20 million ha) of rain forest are cleared each year. Experts predict that, at this rate of destruction, the rain forest will be completely gone by the year 2007. The rain forest is home to more than half the world's animal and plant species. Eighty percent of the

POLLUTION

Some species die out because of **pesticides**. The eggs of certain species of birds that have eaten pesticides become very thin-shelled, and the babies do not survive.

Some species die because the soil and water where they live

and breed have been contaminated by **acid rain**. Acid rain is rain or snow that mixes with air pollution before falling to the ground. It fills the environment with too much acid for plants and animals to survive.

▲ Humans often burn the savanna, prairie, and forest for farmland and urban development.

▲ Oil spilled from ships is deadly to the environment and wildlife.

PREDATORS AND COMPETITORS

Certain wildlife species have become extinct because people introduced **predators** into an area where they did not naturally exist. The environment of Hawaii was drastically changed when people introduced livestock there in the late eighteenth

▲ The Molokai creeper has not been observed for over twenty-five years.

Many types of wildlife die and habitats are destroyed when crude oil spills out of huge tanker ships into the environment. This destruction also occurs when industries dump wastes into bodies of water.

century. The grazing livestock destroyed habitats and many plants. This, in turn, led to native animal extinctions. Native animals also died out because they had to compete with the introduced animals for limited food, water, shelter, and space.

THE POACHING PROBLEM

African and Asian elephants, black rhinoceroses, and many other animals are endangered because of **poaching** and overhunting as well as habitat destruction. Poachers kill elephants for their tusks and rhinoceroses for their horns.

▲ Poachers hunt and kill the magnificent elephants for their tusks.

▲ Passenger pigeons once flew in flocks of millions in eastern North America.

fifteen billion. But, because of overhunting, the bird was extinct by 1914.

Leopards, Bengal and Siberian tigers, the polar bear, and the California condor have been hunted nearly into extinction for sport.

Wildlife are also driven toward extinction by practices such as the collection of animals as pets, for use in zoos, and for various types of research.

Certain animals, such as whales, have been overhunted for the valuable products they provide. Many other species are overhunted for their fur, hide, or feathers.

In the mid-1800s, the passenger pigeon, *Ectopistes migratorius*, was the most common **vertebrate** in North America, numbering about

▲ What will be the fate of the world's animals if they are either killed in the wild or confined to cages?

HONOR AND RESPECT

This planet does not just belong to human beings. We share our environment with approximately thirty million other kinds of creatures. The animals that currently live among us have adapted and survived our changing world for thousands, perhaps even millions, of years. They have a rightful place on Earth. They deserve respect, honor, and the chance to continue to take part in life on this diverse planet. It is their birthright.

Animals that are endangered need human assistance in order to survive. Pushing

▲ Southern Australia is the last refuge of the common stick-nest rat.

17

animals into extinction or sitting idly by while they are disappearing is unacceptable — especially when we know that no species can ever be replaced.

BALANCE OF NATURE

No living being exists on its own. We are all a part of the balance of nature. All plants, animals, and people are part of a fragile system called the **biosphere**. Each living being contributes to the balance of this complex and fragile system.

▲ Even humans cannot survive in areas where resources are scarce.

The biosphere is made up of what are known as **ecosystems**, or the relationships of plants and animals to the environment. Each species is connected to the survival of other species. The loss of any one species upsets the balance of nature. It can set in motion a reaction that negatively affects the survival of all life forms, including humans.

People must stop thinking of themselves as separate from the rest of nature. It is not a struggle of human *against* beast. We are all part of nature, sharing the same environment. We need each other to survive.

▲ Rain forests contain plant and animal species that can provide cures for illness and disease.

SCIENTIFIC REASONS

Each living being has a special chemical make-up that has developed over time. We can learn about many life processes by studying these chemical make-ups. If the animal containing a particular chemistry becomes extinct, all potential benefits are lost.

For instance, valuable medicines have been developed through the study of wildlife. Many prescriptions contain medicines discovered in animals and plants. Many more medicines that could benefit all living things are waiting to be found.

Some farmers practice **biological controls** to increase crop production. Instead of using dangerous, artificial chemicals to control pests, they use insects (such as ladybugs) and other animals that prey on the pests.

Wildlife can also help scientists determine the quality of the environment. If a certain species of fish is dying off, this means there may be something polluting the water. When peregrine falcons, ospreys, and bald eagles began dying a few years ago, it was discovered that the problem was the pesticide DDT. DDT was then banned in the United States because it was proved harmful to all living things.

▲ Instead of spraying pesticides, some farmers use biological controls.

▲ Dozens of fish species are disappearing from fragile aquatic environments.

Animals can provide human beings with a sense of vitality. People become more alive as they witness the beauty and dignity of the animal kingdom. Observing and being with animals helps us feel complete and connected to our world.

▲ About two hundred mountain zebras survive in only a few reserves in Africa.

WILDLIFE CONSERVATION

Wildlife conservation was probably first practiced by the American Indians many years ago. The Indians lived in harmony with the wildlife and plants around them. They did not overhunt animals, taking only what they needed to survive. Then they used every part of the animal, wasting nothing. Native peoples honored, respected, and thanked the animals that gave their lives so their human families could live. All of these practices assured that the animals would be a part of Earth for a long time to come.

▲ This historical drawing depicts two hunters and their prey.

But as Europeans spread their settlements throughout the world, various species of wildlife began to vanish because the settlers did not practice wildlife conservation. During the seventeenth and eighteenth centuries, the British colonists in America passed laws to protect wildlife, but the laws were broken by hunters and trappers. Non-Indians in the United States did not begin practicing wildlife conservation until the late 1800s.

▲ Grand Montagne Reserve on Rodrigues Island in the Indian Ocean.

SAVING HABITAT

During the late 1800s, national parks and wildlife refuges began to be established in the United States. Italy, Canada, Australia, and Africa also created their first wildlife sanctuaries in the mid-to-late 1800s. Asia and South America followed in the early 1900s. Today, there are over 1,200 protected areas throughout the world.

Endangered species can be saved if their habitats are saved. But it is estimated that at least four times the current amount of protected areas need to be established if efforts to save endangered wildlife are to be successful.

ORGANIZATIONS

When the United Nations (UN) was formed in 1945, nations began to work together to conserve wildlife. The UN created the International Union for Conservation of Nature and

▲ The impala is endangered because of hunting by humans.

Natural Resources (IUCN) in 1948 to save endangered species. The IUCN helped set up the World Wildlife Fund in 1961. This organization raises funds that help develop and maintain wildlife and habitat conservation programs throughout the world.

Many private organizations have also been created for wildlife and habitat conservation. In the United States, these include the National Audubon Society and the National Wildlife Federation. A worldwide organization called the Nature Conservancy works with farmers, native tribes, businesses, individuals, and governments to buy and protect natural areas.

LEGISLATION

Many nations have also passed laws to protect wildlife. These laws regulate hunting and fishing; control predators and competitors; and set strict standards for soil, water, and forestry conservation. But, as is the case for the world's rain forests, much more needs to be done.

The United States passed the Endangered Species Act in 1973. This legislation is designed to protect wildlife as well as habitat. The act has been mostly successful. When it was first passed, seventy-eight species were listed as endangered. Many of these species are now stable or increasing, and three have become extinct. Seventeen species on the original list are still declining, so further conservation efforts and a strengthening of the Endangered Species Act are needed.

Many countries are also working to pass laws to protect the environment. In 1972, ninety-one nations signed an agreement to stop dumping toxic materials into the open seas.

CAPTIVE BREEDING

Captive breeding programs may also help save endangered wildlife. If a species is not surviving in the wild, efforts may be necessary to raise the animals

▲ Whales are still hunted, despite an International Whaling Commission ban.

▲ Certain species have become so few in number that individual animals have trouble finding a mate. For this reason, cross-breeding with other species sometimes occurs. The red wolf may die out in its pure form because it has been crossbreeding with coyotes.

in captivity for attempted later release into the wild. For example, conservationists are trying to save the American whooping crane through captive breeding.

BALANCE THE HUMAN POPULATION

In addition, several countries are working to balance the human population with Earth's resources. If the growth of the world's human population continues at its present rate, the day will come when Earth's precious resources will be completely used up.

THE FUTURE

What does the future hold for our wildlife, and ultimately for all of us in the web of life? In spite of today's conservation efforts, the future is uncertain. Continued loss of habitat, increased pollution, poaching, and overhunting — all

▲ A thriving botanical conservatory.

magnified by nonstop human population growth — pose a constant threat to our wild animals and the natural areas where they make their homes. But one thing is certain.

Humans hold the power to see that our wildlife and their habitats survive. It is the responsibility of each of us to do everything possible to help in their struggle to survive.

▲ Experts estimate that within forty years, the world human population will double.

▲ Most of the giant pandas' forest home has been lost. Can the panda be saved?

SCIENTIFIC NAMES OF ANIMALS IN THIS BOOK

Animals have different names in every language. To simplify matters, researchers the world over have agreed to use the same scientific names, usually from ancient Greek or Latin, to identify animals. With this in mind, most animals are classified by two names. One is the genus name; the other is the name of the species to which they belong. Additional names indicate further subgroupings. The scientific names for the animals included in *In Peril: Endangered Wildlife* are:

African elephant	*Loxodonta africanus*
Asian elephant	*Elephas maximus*
Asiatic lion	*Panthera leo persica*
Atlantic salmon	*Salmo salar*
Auroch	*Bos primigenius*
Aye-aye	*Daubentonia madagascariensis*
Bald eagle	*Haliaeetus leucocephalus*
Bengal tiger	*Panthera tigris tigris*
Black rhinoceros	*Rhinoceros unicornis*
Black-footed ferret	*Mustela nigripes*
Blue whale	*Balaenoptera musculus*
Broad-nosed gentle lemur	*Hapalemur simus*
California condor	*Gymnogyps californianus*
California grizzly bear	*Ursus arctos*
Carolina parakeet	*Conuropsis carolinensis*
Common stick-nest rat	*Leporillus conditor*
Dodo	*Raphus cucullatus*
Florida black wolf	*Canis rufus floridanus*
Florida manatee	*Trichechus manatus manatus*
Galápagos turtle	*Chelonoidis abingdoni*

Giant panda	*Ailuropoda melanoleuca*
Great auk	*Pinguinis impennis*
Impala	*Aepyceros melampus pettersi*
Leopard	*Panthera pardus*
Molokai creeper	*Oreomystis flammea*
Mountain gorilla	*Gorilla gorilla*
Mountain zebra	*Equus zebra zebra*
Muriqui	*Brachyteles arachnoides*
Orangutan	*Pongo pygmaeus*
Osprey	*Pandion haliaetus*
Passenger pigeon	*Ectopistes migratorius*
Peregrine falcon	*Falco peregrinus*
Polar bear	*Thalarctos maritimus*
Red kite	*Milvus milvus*
Red wolf	*Canis rufus*
Réunion Island gecko	*Phelsuma inexpectata*
Ruffed lemur	*Varecia variegata*
Siberian tiger	*Panthera tigris altaica*
Stephen Island wren	*Venicus lyalli*
Whooping crane	*Grus americana*

GLOSSARY

acid rain — rain or snow falling through the atmosphere that mixes with pollution from the air.

biological controls — the use of natural processes to achieve a desired result.

biosphere — plants, animals, and people plus the environment in which they live.

captive breeding — the raising of animals in captivity where the resources they need and protection against harm are provided.

ecosystem — the plants, animals, people, and nonliving things that are part of the environment and that affect one another.

endangered — in peril of dying out, or becoming extinct.

extinct — no longer surviving on Earth.

habitat — an environment where plants and animals live and grow.

pesticides — chemicals used to kill insects or rodents.

poaching — killing animals illegally for profit.

predators — animals that kill other animals for food.

reserve — area of land set aside for the protection of animals and plants.

species — a grouping of animals with similar characteristics.

vertebrate — an animal that has a backbone.

wildlife conservation — the effort to preserve and protect wild animals and plants to save them from extinction.

MORE BOOKS TO READ

Close to Extinction. John Burton (Watts)

Ecology Basics. Lawrence Stevens (Prentice Hall)

Endangered Species Means There's Still Time. U.S. Government Printing Office, Washington, D.C.

Fifty Simple Things Kids Can Do to Save the Earth. Earthworks Group (Andrews and McMeel)

Project Panda Watch. Miriam Schlein (Atheneum)

Saving Animals: The World Wildlife Book of Conservation. Bernard Stonehouse (Macmillan)

Why Are Animals Endangered? Isaac Asimov (Gareth Stevens)

VIDEOTAPES

Call or visit your local library or video rental store to see if these videotapes are available for your viewing.

African Wildlife. (National Geographic)

Animals Are Beautiful People. Jamie Uys (Pro Footage Library - America's Wildlife)

PLACES TO WRITE

The following organizations work to educate people about animals, promote the protection of animals, and encourage the conservation of their environments. If you write for more information, be sure to state clearly what you want to know.

Wildlife Conservation
   International
185th Street and Southern
   Boulevard
Bronx, New York 10460

Canadian Wildlife
   Federation
2740 Queensview Drive
Ottawa, Ontario
K2B 1A2

International Wildlife
   Coalition
P.O. Box 461
Port Credit Postal Station
Mississauga, Ontario
L5G 4M1

New South Wales National
   Parks and Wildlife
   Service Info. Centre
43 Bridge Street
(P.O. Box 1967)
Hurstville NSW 2220
Australia

Conservation Commission
   of the Northern
   Territory
P.O. Box 496
Palmerston
NT 0831
Australia

National Audubon Society
700 Broadway
New York, New York
10003

ACTIVITIES TO HELP SAVE ENDANGERED SPECIES

1. Write the United States Department of the Interior, Publications Unit, Fish and Wildlife Service, Washington, D.C., 20240, for a list of endangered wildlife. Then write to government officials and express your support for the protection of these animals and their habitats. Also, write to government officials to express your support of strengthening the Endangered Species Act.

2. Contact a nature organization in your area. Ask how you can become involved in helping save wildlife.

3. Do not buy wild or exotic animals as pets. Also, do not buy fur, bearskin rugs, ivory, or any other products that endanger animals.

4. Visit a national wildlife refuge. Volunteer to help out on special projects at a refuge in your area.

5. Educate your friends about respecting wildlife. Ask them not to participate in acts of carelessness or cruelty that could injure an animal.

INDEX